# FLAK

## A PHOTO STUDY OF GERMAN ANTI-AIRCRAFT WEAPONS

# CONTENTS

**PHOTO CREDITS**
The photos in this book come from a wide variety of sources, including the US National Archives, the USAF, the USMC Historical Division, the Patton Museum, the US Army Ordnance Museum, SA-Kuva, and the author's collection. Other photo contributions are specifically noted and gratefully appreciated.

**FLAK**
© Canfora Publishing 2024
ISBN 978-91-988425-2-4
Design: Toni Canfora
Print: Printbest, Estonia

Canfora Publishing
Industrivägen 19
171 48 Solna, Stockholm, Sweden
www.canfora.se, info@canfora.se

# INTRODUCTION

Shortly after the earliest aircraft became "warplanes" during World War One, the poor bloody and muddy infantry were obliged to find some defense against their airborne tormentors. The Kaiser's army was quick to develop anti-aircraft systems, ranging from simple adaptations of infantry machine guns firing upwards from the trenches, to sophisticated self-propelled AA cannons. Germany's FlaK ("Fliegerabwehrkanone")* forces were born of necessity, and performed with deadly efficiency. Allied flyers in WWI called German AA fire "Archie" and "Flaming Onions". By WWII, everyone had settled on the term "Flak".

By 1917, the capabilities and even the amount of Allied ground attack aircraft had increased to such a level that the German army had to respond. Beyond dedicating more machine guns to anti-aircraft duty, the Kaiser's men created mobile AA platforms to quickly move Flak cannons to where they were needed most—mobile Flak was sent to cover troop concentrations, transportation centers, artillery positions, and observation balloons. Early Flak gunners were faced with an incredible challenge in determining the range to and speed of their targets, but even their improvised AA weapons were inflicting significant casualties on Allied trench-strafers, low-le-

From the beginning of German AA defense, the MG08 proved an effective weapon against low-flying aircraft. This example uses a clamp mount to create an expedient AA pedestal.

Mobile flak in WWI: The 7.7cm Leichte Kraftwagengeschutze M1914 in action in Flanders during August 1917.

*Also known as Flugabwehrkanone

vel bombers, and recon aircraft. By the middle of 1917, German AA weapons had greatly increased in caliber and efficiency, with cannons like the 88mm "K-Flak" firing ten shells per minute, up to 20,000 feet. Accordingly, the number of rounds for each flak kill fell from 11,588 in 1915 to just 5,040 in 1918. By the end of the war on the Western Front, German AA gunners claimed 1,588 Allied aircraft of all types. Flak was a significant force to be reckoned with.

The end of the Great War and the hard economic times that followed didn't prevent German designers from developing new flak weapons to keep pace with the fast-evolving aircraft types. By the late 1930s, the Germans had mated their effective 2 cm Flak 30 to the light Sd. Kfz. 10 halftrack, and later to the Panzer I chassis, and the concept of the Flakpanzer was born.

During the blitzkrieg era of 1939-1941, the Wehrmacht's mobile flak provided much more protection for the fast-advancing troops than what it is given credit for. Throughout the invasion of Western Europe in 1940, flak units claimed 854 Allied aircraft shot down as well as 300 armored vehicles destroyed. The flak troops' success continued during the invasion of the Soviet Union, with nearly 5,300 aircraft and 1,900 armored vehicles destroyed by the end of 1941. In the blitzkrieg years, French, British, or Soviet aircraft were never able to break through the flak umbrella to seriously threaten German forces.

As WWII continued, Flak weapons continued to grow and diversify. In the early war period, rifle-caliber machine guns and 20mm auto-cannons were sufficient to defend against low-level attacks by Allied aircraft.

Flak mobility was always a prime concern: This is a Daimler Anti-Aircraft Armored Carrier equipped with Krupp 7.1 cm L/28 AA gun, Model 1909.

The first 88mm flak gun: The 8.8cm Flak 16, or "K-flak" demonstrated during the summer of 1917.

As the tactical situation changed—German troops had to combat growing attacks by ever-more heavily armed (and often armored) Allied ground attack aircraft. Single 20mm guns grew into quadruple mounts, and more and more 37mm guns appeared in both ground and mobile mounts. The anti-aircraft arms race proceeded at an incredible pace. A significant portion of the World War II air war over Europe and the Mediterranean was a Flak war.

By late 1942, as the RAF and USAAF heavy bombers began to strike targets within Occupied Europe and inside the Reich, the nature of Germany's flak defenses began to change. Tasked with protecting industrial centers, the heavy guns of the strategic flak defenses grew exponentially. Ranging from 88mm up to 128mm, Germany's heavy flak was dedicated to protecting critical metropolitan areas within the greater Reich: Berlin

was defended by 440 heavy flak guns, Hamburg had about 400, Vienna had 320, and Munich nearly 300. Berlin's guns were supported by up to 250 searchlights. At the critically important Ploesti oil fields, the Germans emplaced 36 heavy batteries (mostly 88mm) and 16 light batteries (20mm and 37mm)—the skies were filled with anti-aircraft fragments.

As the war progressed, Flak crews declined in age and experience as Germany combed through its personnel to find more combat troops. After

Covering the blitzkrieg: The Sd. Kfz. 10/4 along with towed 2 cm AA guns provided effective defense against low-flying Allied bombers during the blitz era.

The powerful and fast-firing 3.7 cm Flak 43 debuted in 1944. As Allied aircraft began to rule the skies, there were never enough of these weapons.

An 8,8 cm flak battery in the field:  The 8,8 cm battery was normally equipped with three to six guns, plus two or three 2 cm guns for local protection. In this case, ammunition storage is built into the sides of the rectangular dug in position. Most 8,8 cm flak positions had two entrances. Bunkers for the crew were built within a short distance of the gun, along with a command post and a searchlight position. A second gun can be seen in the background.

1943, German flak crews used more and more women, older men, and early teen boys on the guns, and with foreign workers and POWs as ammunition passers. The "flak helpers", (Flakhelfer-male or Flakhelferin-female) steadily grew in number, and by April 1945 civilians and auxiliaries made up 44% of the flak crews.

Meanwhile, the greatly increased number of guns led to ammunition shortages and by early 1944 flak crews were forced to restrict their firing. By 1945, the Germans were only able to deliver about half of the firepower that their total number of guns could have provided. Yet even despite the shortages and the ever-decreasing number of trained flak crews, German flak grew in effectiveness throughout the war. As the successes of German interceptors decreased, flak kills increased. German estimates in 1944 showed that flak accounted for nearly one third of all Allied aircraft shot down, as well as two-thirds of all those damaged. Also in 1944, the Germans reckoned that it took about 8,000 flak shells (of all types) fired to destroy one Allied bomber—it was a deadly numbers game, and the Reich could not produce enough anti-aircraft ammunition to win.

As a result, even though Germany's flak weapons often inflicted serious casualties on Allied bombers, they were never able to turn the attackers away, or prevent them from coming back.

The USAAF lost 18,418 aircraft in the war against Germany, with 7,821 considered destroyed by anti-aircraft fire, nearly 43% of the total. That total could have been much higher, and German flak was held back not by manpower, number of cannons, or by ammunition production—as they were

"Flak so thick you could walk on it!" Once committed to their bomb run, there was little the bombers could do but endure the intensity of the AA barrage.

by the technology of their shell fuses. Technological advances had increased flak efficiency from 1941 onwards, including gun-laying radar and greater fragmentation of the ammunition—leading to a 3x increase in efficiency by German estimates. In late 1944, the Germans introduced a "double fuse", that exploded on contact and also by timing. These fuses increased the effectiveness of 88mm guns by 5x, 105mm guns by 3x, and 128mm guns by 2x. But these successes obscure Germany's failure to develop a "proximity fuse". The efficiency of the proximity fuse was demonstrated by the ability of the British 3.7-inch and US 90mm AA guns to regularly destroy the fast-moving V-1 robot bombs in 1944-45. A postwar USAAF study concluded that if the German flak had used proximity fuses, they would have increased efficiency by a factor of 3.4 across the board. Lost in the ongoing discussions of jet fighters, air-to-air missiles, and cannon-armed interceptors, that level of flak effectiveness might well have blunted the entire Allied strategic bombing campaign by itself.

During September 1942, the Germans began to work on anti-aircraft rockets. Their concepts fell into two categories—unguided and guided (via radio-control). Despite advanced rocket technology, none of the AA rockets were successful. The unguided types were intended to be ripple-fired. 30-50 at a time, in a shotgun effect. The Foehn (3.3 pounds, 3600 foot range) was a low-altitude weapon against strafing aircraft, and the Taifun (65 pounds, 52,000 foot range) was intended for use against heavy bomber formations.

Flak is credited with bringing down more than 7,800 USAAF aircraft, including this B-26 Marauder of the 344th Bomb Group (Medium), hit over Germany during early 1945.

The four radio guided AA rockets consisted of the Enzian (660 pound warhead), Rheintochter (330 pound warhead), Schmetterling (51 pound warhead), and Wasserfall (200 pound warhead). All of these designs look impressive for the era, but they all failed to reliably reach a bomber formation, and reliably explode anywhere close to their targets. The German rockets may have been capable, but the necessary radio-control technology and proximity fuses were not. But the German experiments opened the door, and postwar developments in Western nations and in the Soviet Union gave us the highly advanced AA missile systems now in service around the world.

Several attempts were made to mount the 88mm flak to a tracked platform, but none reached series production. This is a prototype of the Sonderfahrgestell (Pz.Sfl.IVc).

The failed experiment: German radio-controlled AA rocket concepts, including Rheintochter (top) and the Enzian (bottom) were abandoned after they could not be successfully guided into Allied bomber formations.

## US Army Flak review

The US Army review titled "German Anti-Aircraft Artillery" (published in February 1943) provides an excellent wartime perspective on Flak innovations and modifications—and on the developing trends that would define Germany's AA weapons during the last two years of the war.

*With the tremendous strides in development of combat aviation during the period between World War I and World War II, it became increasingly evident that a corresponding development of AA materiel and tactics was quite necessary. Although the Germans were limited in their military establishment as a result of World War I, they nevertheless conducted extensive research and tests to develop new AA materiel. During this post-war period, also came experiments with mechanized armored vehicles, and new doctrine as to the possibilities of their employment. Under*

*the circumstances, it was only logical that some experimentation should take place with the object of designing a gun which could be used against either aircraft or ground vehicles. In 1936 the Spanish Civil War gave the Germans a chance to test their first efforts along these lines; then in 1939 the campaign in Poland permitted a full test of the refined product, and results were used as a guide on which to base standardization and further development. The later campaign in France and other campaigns have, of course, served as further proving grounds.*

*One of the main results of the battle experiences of the Germans has vindicated the concept that AA guns used outside of purely static positions must be highly mobile, and that even in static situations it is to the best interests of protection against hostile aircraft to have a certain proportion of the AA artillery defenses in a highly mobile state for purposes of flexibility. Furthermore, the in-*

One of the keys to the success of Germany's flak weapons was their adaptability, and their good performance against ground targets.

creased use of AA weapons with mobile units in the field has given a great spur to development of AA mobility and dual-purpose weapon construction.

With the practical tests of 1936 in the Spanish Civil War came the realization that with some modifications the then current AA weapons would have definite possibilities as effective antitank weapons. This finding was even more acceptable in view of the German military precept of acting on the offense wherever possible. The possibility of employing AA guns in forward areas in an offensive role removed them from the status of defensive weapons and placed them in the category of important offensive weapons. The Polish Campaign, the French Campaign, and the early successes of Rommel in the Libyan Desert are eloquent proof of the increasing development and use of AA weapons against mechanized ground targets. It should be remembered, of course, that AA gunnery demands weapons with a high rate of fire, rapid fire-control calculation, fast tracking speeds, and a high muzzle velocity.

These factors contributed to the decision to adapt these weapons to an AT role. The original difficulty in making these AA weapons dual purpose rested mainly in securing a satisfactory mobile carriage or mount which could withstand equally well the shock and recoil of high-elevation AA fire, and of horizontal and sub-horizontal fire. With satisfactory development and use of the AA gun as an AT weapon came the logical discovery that the main AA/AT weapons could be used against targets other than aircraft or tanks.

We hear of the 88-mm guns being used against fortified gun positions, as well as for the direct support of ground troops, for interdiction fire against enemy communications, and for fire against river and coastal targets. As a result of these and similar experiences, German field commanders have found AA artillery to be one of their most useful weapons, and there is evidence of a trend suggesting that German artillery of the future, up to a certain caliber, will include an even greater proportion of AA weapons placed on multipurpose mounts.

The classic 88mm Flak 36: While the "88" won considerable fame in the anti-tank role, it was also one of the deadliest anti-aircraft weapons of WWII.

# 7.92mm Machine Guns

Beginning in the early days of World War One, German troops found ways to use their machine guns in the anti-aircraft role. The water-cooled MG08 quickly proved to be an effective AA gun against aircraft flying below 5,000 feet, fed by a 250-round belt, and cycling at 500 rounds per minute. Specialized AA sights were developed by the mid-war period, and these were attached to the water jacket of the MG08 and later MG08/15. Various mounts were configured on wooden or metal posts, and machine gunners learned the fine art of combating enemy aircraft. A key lesson learned was that the belt-feeding mechanism was not strong enough to pull through a dangling ammo belt, and the loader needed to manually assist the fabric belt into the gun, ensuring there were jam-causing kinks. As aircraft speeds increased, so too did the need for faster-firing machine guns.

At the beginning of World War II, the Wehrmacht had the new MG34 general purpose machine gun in service, along with the MG13 and the WWI hold-over MG08/15. The MG34 cycled at about 900 rounds per minute, making it an excellent AA weapon for the infantry, and was used in this role throughout the war. The MG34 was fed by 50 and 250-round belts, as well as by a 75-round "saddle drum" magazine.

The later MG42 cycled at an exceptionally high rate—about 1,200 rpm. While this a benefit in some ways, the MG42 normally needed the assistant gunner to ensure that the fast-moving metal link ammo belt did not kink or jam.

German transports, particularly trains and truck convoys, were always in great need of AA protection, and this often outstripped the available numbers of MG34s and MG42s. Consequently, many older machine guns (MG08s, MG08/15s, MG13s, and MG15s), along with captured Polish, French, Czech, and Soviet MGs were pressed into service as light AA weapons. Guns like the MG13 and French FM 24/29 (20-round and 25-round magazines), and the MG15 (75-round drum) were restricted in sustained fire due to their small ammunition capacity. Regardless, the demand for light AA weapons was extreme, and German troops used whatever MGs were available until the end of the war. As Allied ground attack aircraft flew faster and carried greater armor protection, the effectiveness of rifle-caliber MGs was significantly reduced. Even so, German machine guns blazed away at airborne attackers until the bitter end.

The simplest form of mobile flak: The WWI-vintage MG08 on its "Sled 08" tripod, fitted with a pedestal anti-aircraft adapter. The water-cooled MG08 cycled at 500 rounds per minute and was normally fed with a 250-round fabric belt.

The older MG08/15 was often mounted on the 08/15 AA tripod and used for light flak duty.

Formerly a defensive gun carried by Luftwaffe bombers, many MG 15s were used in the AA role. The cyclic rate was 1,000 rpm, and the gun was fed by 75-round saddle drum magazines. This MG 15 retains its "catch bag" for spent casings, while the assistant stabilizes the tripod.

13

The MG 13 was an early general purpose machine gun that gave way to the MG 34. Even so, the MG 13 soldiered on in reserve roles, particularly as a light AA gun. A 25-round box magazine was the normal feed device, but some AA MGs used a 75-round "saddle drum". Cyclic rate was 600 rpm.

The MG 34 on the Lafette 34 tripod, using the tubular AA elevator. The spider-web "speed sight" anti-aircraft sight is fitted. (Petr Dolezal)

The MG 34 was an excellent anti-aircraft MG, with strong cyclic rate of 900 rpm. The example to the right uses the simple Dreibein 34 AA tripod (with telescoping legs). Note the details on the AA sight and the 250-round disintegrating link ammo belt.

In some cases, the MG 34 was the only available anti-aircraft defense gun. This one is seen protecting German troops against Soviet air attacks in Finland. *(SA-Kuva)*

The "Maschinengewehrwagen 36"— a two wheeled cart with pneumatic tires, fitted with the Zwillingsockel 36 AA mount.

The Zwillingsockel 36 was an excellent light AA mount that offered a good amount of firepower during the early war years. *(Petr Dolezal)*

Mobile AA support: The Maschinengewehrwagen 36 were often drawn by horses during the blitzkrieg years.

"Hitler's Buzzsaw" in the anti-aircraft role: The MG 42 mounted on the Dreibein 34 AA tripod. (Fama, France et Atlantic/Archives Calvados)

The MG34 "Zwilling" mounted in the rear of a Stoewer Le.Gl.Einheitz-Pkw Kfz.4.

Although the MG 42 cycled at 1,200 rounds per minute, the wild movement of the 250-round ammunition belt required special attention so that it did not kink and jam the gun.

On some late production examples of the Panzerjäger Tiger Ausf. B Jagdtiger, an MG 42 AA gun was mounted on a pedestal atop the engine deck.

# 15/20mm MG 151

The Mauser MG 151 *Maschinengewehr* series of autocannons were designed as aircraft armament, with the initial MG 151 (chambered in 15.1 mm caliber, using the 15x96mm cartridge) debuting in 1940. Due to a need for greater explosive power, the original 15 mm variant was replaced in Luftwaffe service by a 20 mm type known as the MG 151/20. The surplus 15 mm guns (renamed MG 151/15) were allocated for anti-aircraft use, normally appearing in single mounts, and later in the war as triple ("Drilling") mounts.

The effective range of the MG 151/15 was about 3,000 feet, with a cyclic rate of up to 750 rounds per minute. Each gun weighed 80 pounds and was 6.75 feet long. Ammunition was fed by disintegrating link belts, and while the high cyclic rate was useful for anti-aircraft work, it also quickly exhausted the on-board ammunition of self-propelled mounts.

The triple guns were mounted on pedestal, with tall ammunition cannisters grouped underneath, and the weapon was aimed and fired by a single gunner. The Drilling was mounted on the Sd. Kfz. 251/21 "Drilling" half-track, various light vehicles, as well as large trailers (including the Sonderanhänger Ost 1.5t trailer). Another important mount for the triple autocannons was aboard flak trains—with some Drilling housed in large circular turrets made of reinforced concrete. By 1945, the triple gun mounts also included MG 151/20 cannons.

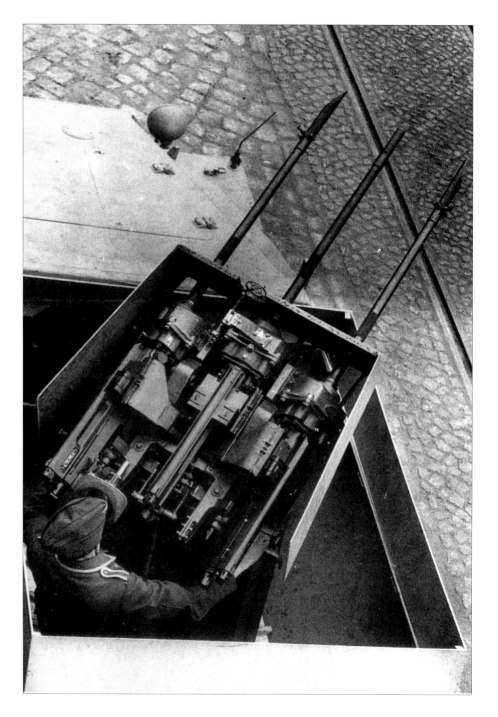

A good overhead view of the triple MG 151/15 mount carried by the Sd. Kfz. 251/21 halftrack.

American troops examine a collection of triple mounted MG 151/15 guns in Cologne during the spring of 1945. These weapons were the main armament of the Sd. Kfz. 251/21. (*NARA*)

20mm MG 151/20s mounted in circular concrete casemates (8-inches thick). The triple flak guns are mounted on a concrete pedestal in the center of the tower. *(NARA)*

Two views of a smashed Sd. Kfz. 251/21 on the Western Front in late 1944. Note the details of the gun mount and the cramped fighting compartment of the vehicle. (*NARA*)

A triple MG 151/15 mounted on a Sonderanhänger Ost 1.5t trailer, captured in Germany during the spring of 1945. (*NARA*)

# 20mm FLAK 30/38

The origins of the German 2 cm flak guns date back to World War One. During the Great War, Germany produced the Becker 2 cm Type M2 auto-cannon, and the Becker would become the basis for the famous Oerlikon 20mm gun, one of the most effective and long-serving light AA guns of all time. While Switzerland's SEMAG produced their improved Becker design as the Oerlikon, Germany's Rheinmetall sought to produce their version of the 2 cm AA weapon, even though this was forbidden by the terms of the Treaty of Versailles. Rheinmetall circumvented the legal logjam by selling the 2 cm "Flak 28" to Switzerland's Solothurn (which was owned by Rheinmetall). Solothurn proceeded to make a new 2 cm AA weapon called the ST-5, which leveraged the powerful 20x138mm round, sometimes called the "Long Solothurn". Eventually, the ST-5 became the Flak 30.

While the new Flak 30 autocannon was adaptable and powerful, the weapon suffered from a low cyclic rate (about 120 rounds per minute)—exacerbated by the gun's small 20-round magazine capacity. The problem of a low magazine capacity lingered, even as Rheinmetall improved the weapon with the Flak 38 (adopted by the Wehrmacht and Kriegsmarine in 1939). Though the Flak 38 was lighter in weight, and cycled at a respectable 220 rpm, the undersized 20-round magazine remained in use throughout the war.

Even so, the Flak 30/38 offered additional uses—particularly as an anti-tank weapon during the 1930s and the early WWII era. Basic armor-piercing ammunition (PanzergranatpatroneL'spur) for the 20x138mm round could penetrate 20mm of armor at 100 meters, and 15mm out to 500 meters. The Solothurn ST-5/Flak 30 guns were credited with AFV kills during the Spanish Civil War (used by Nationalist forces) and during the Sino-Japanese War (used by Chinese forces). During WWII, the Panzergranatpatrone 40 round was developed with a tungsten-carbide core and was capable of penetrating 39mm of armor at about 100 meters.

Most of the Flak 38 guns were towed into position by a wide range of vehicles aboard the Sd. Ah. 52 trailer. The gun commander and 5-man crew could also manhandle the gun (and fire it) on the trailer for short distances if required. As the need for mobile flak grew to unprecedented proportions, the Flakpanzer I, Flakpanzer 38(t), the Sd. Kfz. 251/17, Sd. Kfz. 10/4 & 10/5, and various heavy trucks carried the single 20mm guns into combat. At sea, the Flak 38 was mounted aboard a wide range of Kriegsmarine vessels, including U-boats.

The Flak 30/38 could be elevated up to a maximum of 90 degrees. The gun captain at the rear left uses a Stereoscopic Rangefinder Model 1936. Note the 20-round magazine inserted at the lower right. This gun has the later "Linealvisier 38" ring sight.

A 2 cm Flak 30 set up to cover a bridge on the Eastern Front.

An excellent profile view of a 2 cm Flak 38 captured by US troops in North Africa during 1943. (*NARA*)

The gunner's seat and the left side of the Flakvisier 35.

The reflector sight of the Flakvisier 35 (top right). Note the 20-round magazine at bottom center. *(Petr Dolezal)*

Young crewmen with their Flak 38 gun, providing air defense for a supply train. An Opel Olympia can be seen on the flatcar in the background. *(Petr Dolezal)*

A cheerful looking Luftwaffe Flak crew in Finland, 1941. This photo offers a good view of the firing pedal and aiming device of the Flak 30 as well as the elevation wheel. It usually took a crew of five to operate the gun with maximum effectiveness. (SA-Kuva)

Finnish forces also made extensive use of German weapons. The crew of this Flak 30 has taken position on high ground, with a clear line of fire and a good overview of the terrain and airspace. It was not an easy task to dig these positions in frozen soil. (*SA-Kuva*)

A beautiful view of another Flak 30 in Finnish service on the island of Suursaari in the Gulf of Finland. 50 Flak 30s were delivered from Germany in 1939.

The Flak 38 on its trailer in travel position. This weapon was captured in Germany during the spring of 1945. *(NARA)*

An American collection point for 2 cm flak guns captured in Germany in early 1945. The Flak 38 at left is missing its flash hider. *(NARA via Darren Neely)*

Several 2 cm flak guns in a graveyard full of captured German artillery in Normandy. Flak 30 and Flak 38 models are mixed together — with a Flak 38 in the foreground and a 8.8 cm Raketenwerfer 43 "Puppchen" immediately behind it. In the distance, a pair of 8.8 cm flak guns can be seen. *(NARA)*

The 2 cm flak guns went into combat in a variety of ways: Aboard a Mercedes-Benz L3000, mounted on a captured Soviet ZIS-5 truck, and below, towed by an Opel Blitz.

Abandoned German equipment in Finland, 1944. This Flak 30 is towed by a Kfz. 15 (Horch 901) on its Sonderanhänger 51. A PaK 40 can be seen in the background. *(SA-Kuva)*

This white-washed Flak 30 is towed by a Krupp Protze, somewhere on the Eastern Front. The harsh weather took its toll on men and machines alike, and made gun maintenance and readiness particularly challenging. Note "kill marks" on the gun shield. (BPK Bildagentur)

Improvised mobile flak: a Krupp-Protze Kfz. 81 armed with a 2 cm Flak 30 cannon. Seen outside Riga, summer 1941.

This factory fresh Sd.Kfz 10/4 features the Flak 38, which began replacing the Flak 30 on this vehicle from early 1941. It lacks the gun shield and protective covers for the Mauser 98k rifle racks on the front fenders, introduced in 1942. The Sd.Kfz 10/5 was also introduced that year, with a wider platform for the Flak 38. *(Petr Dolezal)*

Sd. Kfz. 10/4 advances into Russia. Note the recognition flag on the hood as well as the Mauser Karabiner 98k rifles strapped to the front fenders. Towed behind is the ammunition trailer (Sd.Ah. 51) that carried up to 640 20mm rounds, the gun sights and rangefinder, and the crew's personal gear.

The Sd. Kfz. 10/5 provided excellent mobile AA coverage through the blitzkrieg era. Note the details of the gun mount, crew positions, and the folding side panels.

A good view of the folding mesh side plates and the attached containers for 20-round magazines. Note the range finder at the bottom right corner, as well as the Pz.Kpfw. III in the background. (*Petr Dolezal*)

An excellent view of the Sd. Kfz. 10/5. The man at the far left holds a traffic control paddle. Note the lack of a gun shield on the 2 cm Flak 30 cannon. The ready ammunition bins attached to the side panels held one 20-round magazine per bin.

A dug in Sd. Kfz. 10/5 on the Russian Front. Note the details on the Z.F. 3x8 optical sight for use against ground targets.

The Sd. Kfz. 10/4 continued to serve throughout the war. The special single-axle ammunition trailer (Sd.Ah. 51-Sonderanhänger) was a critical piece of gear. Note the heavy winter uniforms of the crew. Russian Front, winter 1944.

The trigger mechanism of the Flak 38 was pedal-actuated, providing either full-automatic (450 rpm cyclic, 180 rpm practical) or semi-automatic fire.

Loading the 20x138mmB rounds into 20-round magazines was a time-consuming, thumb-busting chore.

Providing AA protection in any kind of weather. Note the details of the gun shield and the cold-weather gear of the crewman.

Despite their lack of armor, the light flak vehicles often operated in the infantry support role. Note the stick grenades wired to the gun shield of the 2 cm Flak 38.

A Sd. Kfz. 10/5 loaded onto a flatbed railcar. This photo offers a good view of the sheet metal covered rifle racks on the front fender. The vehicle is finished in overall Dunkelgelb (Dark Yellow), as per the directive from February 1943, to replace the Dunkelgrau (Dark Grey) as standard colour. *(Petr Dolezal)*

US troops examine the details of a Sd.Kfz 10/4 captured in North Africa. This vehicle has the later Flak 38 fitted, so it could be an early Sd. Kfz.10/5, although it seems to be lacking the rifle racks fitted to all 10/5s and later model 10/4s. The flatbed of the 10/4 needed to be modified to incorporate the Flak 38. *(NARA)*

Canadian troops with a captured Sd. Kfz. 10/5. Normandy, summer 1944.

The Sd. Kfz. 10/5 continued to serve until the bitter end. This vehicle was captured by US troops in Germany in the late spring of 1945. Note the collection of ammo boxes and the MG34 dangling from the rear. *(NARA)*

A good view of the extremely limited protection that the armored cab provided—covering the radiator, windshield, and the sides of the driver's compartment of the Sd. Kfz. 10/5. (*NARA*)

This Sd. Kfz. 10/5 came to an unfortunate end at the hands of the 90th Infantry Division in Mainz, Germany in the spring of 1945. (The photo has been deliberately blurred to obscure the corpse). *(NARA)*

One of the rare (about 20 built) "2 cm Flak 38 auf Sd. Kfz. 251" conversions. These flakpanzers were created by equipping Sd. Kfz. 251 Ausf. C halftracks with hinged side plates, that provided the 2 cm gun 360-degree traverse. Note the heavy gun smoke from firing the Flak 38.

A wrecked Sd. Kfz. 251/17 serves as a worktable for a GI cleaning his M1 Carbine. The 251/17 fitted with a 2 cm Flak 38 on a pedestal mount (three feet to the rear of the driver's seat)—it is equipped with a small shield (11mm armor) for the gunner. The gun has 360-degree traverse, with -5 to 60-degree elevation. *(NARA)*

The tiny Flakpanzer I. Developed too late to see service in France, the Flakpanzer I saw brief service on the Eastern Front. One of the rarest of all German AFVs, less than 30 of these vehicles were converted by Stoewer. Note the Panzer I ammunition carrier to the left.

With the 2 cm Flak 38 mounted, there was little room aboard the Flakpanzer I for the crew. Ammunition was normally carried in the Sonderanhänger 51 trailer as seen here. *(Petr Dolezal)*

Factory-fresh: A good view of the Flakpanzer 38(t) at BMM production facility in Prague during 1944. 141 of these vehicles were made. *(VUA via Panzerwrecks)*

Camouflaged Flakpanzer 38(t)s (probably 12. SS Division) on the move in Normandy during the summer of 1944. *(Fama, France et Atlantic/Archives Calvados)*

A knocked out Flakpanzer 38(t) in the streets of Torigni Sur Vire, France, August 3, 1944.

# 20MM FLAKVIERLING 38

By the end of the 1930s, military aircraft were gaining speed and offensive capability. Wehrmacht planners saw that their 2cm AA weapons, although capable, were in danger of being overwhelmed by a new generation of bombers. German air defense experts were already looking to upgrade their weapons to 3.7cm guns—delivering a punch many times more powerful at a far greater range. Even though 37mm AA guns were used in ever-increasing numbers, there were never enough to meet the demands of the flak troops. Consequently, Rheinmetall introduced an upgraded variant of the Flak 38, the "2 cm Flakvierling 38", mounting four barrels on a central rotating platform. The new Flakvierling began to appear in service during late 1940.

Despite its powerful appearance, the Flakvierling was simply a coupling of four individual Flak 38 guns into one mount. The cannons do not fire any faster, nor do they have any other capabilities than a standard single-barrel Flak 38. The quadruple grouping makes the individual barrels quicker and easier to load and puts their concentrated firepower under the control of a single gunner. However, the same underlying shortcomings of the single-barrel Flak 38 still apply—particularly the low capacity of the 20-round magazine feed.

To achieve the Flakvierling's maximum rate of fire, per gun (times four), the loaders would have to work at an insane pace, changing out magazines about every six seconds on each gun to reach 1,400 rounds per minute. While theoretically possible, the barrels would be overheated and worn out, and available magazines would be emptied. Sustained fire over a long period is almost guaranteed to overheat the weapon, cause a jam, or even a barrel explosion. In practice, the gunner kept the firing rate down to about 50 rounds per minute per gun—sometimes firing in the semi-automatic mode. The gunner triggered the Flakvierling with two firing pedals, each pedal firing two barrels in opposite corners.

The Flakvierling was produced in significant numbers and served on every major front, including at sea. Its effective range against aircraft was up to 2,200 meters (about 7,200 feet). A few hits from a 2 cm were usually enough to bring down (or cripple) a single-engine fighter. However, armored aircraft like the Ilyushin IL-2 Sturmovik, or particularly sturdy fighter-bombers like the Republic P-47 Thunderbolt were better able to survive 2 cm strikes. The Flakvierling was mounted on several vehicles, most notably the Sd.Kfz. 7/1 halftrack, and the Flakpanzer IV Wirbelwind. When used against ground targets the Flakvierling could effectively reach out to 5,700 meters, and the 2 cm ammunition was highly effective against enemy infantry, light AFVs, and soft-skin vehicles.

On the lookout for Soviet "Jabos", this Sd. Kfz. 7/1 crewman stands watch by the vehicle's 2 cm Flakvierling 38, dug into a field of sunflowers.

A Luftwaffe 2 cm Flakvierling 38 dug in to cover a waterway. The crewman standing in the middle holds a Model 1936 Stereoscopic rangefinder (Enfernungsmesser R36). *(Petr Dolezal)*

All branches of the German military used the Flakvierling 38. This example is seen in action in southern Russia during 1943.

The 2 cm Flakvierling 38 was towed aboard the Sd. Ah. 52 trailer. Note how the armored gun shield folds neatly around the quad gun mount. *(USAHEC via Panzerwrecks)*

In every combat theater, and whatever the weather, the Flakvierlings and their crews provided highly effective flak coverage against low-flying enemy attackers. This weapon has been hastily set up on the Eastern Front.

Waiting for the dreaded "Jabos" to appear. Note the two 20-round magazines visible on the lower left of the gun mount.

Eastern Front, March 1944. A battle hardened Sd.Kfz 7/1crew wearing a mix of uniforms, seen during a lull in the fighting. The gun shield has been thoroughly white-washed. *(BPK Bildagentur)*

A Kfz.410 mittlerer Flakkraftwagen (on a Büssing-NAG 4500A chassis) fitted with a Flakvierling 38 in Normandy. Allied air superiority forced the Germans to use extensive camouflage and to move mostly by night whenever possible. *(Transocean-Europapress/Archives Calvados)*

A Sd. Kfz. 7/1 towing its Sd. Ah. 56 special trailer. When on the move, ammunition storage was normally divided between thirty 20-round magazines carried in the half-track, and ninety 20-round magazines carried in the trailer. *(Petr Dolezal)*

An Sd. Kfz 7/1 with a full crew. Note the Sd. Ah. 56 supply trailer, and the double shield on vehicle's radiator. The vehicle appears to be finished in factory Dunkelgelb all over, and possibly a faded field-applied white-wash on top. *(Petr Dolezal)*

Sd. Kfz 7/1s on the long and winding road deeper into Russia. The vehicle in the background tows a Sd. Ah 56 supply trailer.

A Sd. Kfz. 7/1 of an SS unit, dug in on the Eastern Front. Emplaced like this and well camouflaged, the Flakvierling 38 has a clear field of fire to dominate the area.

A Sd. Kfz. 7/1 with a lightly armored cab, captured by US troops in France during the summer of 1944. The Flakvierling 38 quadruple mount is missing one of its barrels, held by the GI in the left rear corner of the vehicle. Note the empty storage bins for five 20-round magazines visible just below the gun shield. (*NARA*)

An excellent view of the Sd. Kfz. 7/1, showing details of the Flakvierling 38 and mount. This vehicle belonged to Panzerjägerabteilung 256 and was captured and examined by troops of the US Third Army in Germany during early April 1945.

The lightly armored cab of the vehicle seen on Page 74. Note the vision ports and the escape hatch in the cab roof.

Top right: The support and holding jack for the rear outrigger of the quad 2 cm mount.

Right: The support and holding jack for the right front outrigger of the quad 2 cm mount.

The price of failure: Two Flakpanzer IV "Wirbelwind" wrecked and abandoned after the Battle of the Bulge. Note that the Flakpanzer IV in the foreground has burned, and the fire scorched the building beside it. (*NARA*)

A US Army Signal Corps cameraman films a wrecked Flakpanzer IV near Metz, France during late 1944. The 16mm armor plates of the nine-sided, open-top turret are badly damaged at the upper edges, possibly indicating that the flakpanzer lost a duel with a strafing fighter-bomber. (*NARA*)

A camouflaged Flakpanzer IV "Wirbelwind" in France during the summer of 1944. Total production of this vehicle is unclear, but it is unlikely to have exceeded 125 units in total. (*Panzerwrecks*)

Flakpanzer IV "Wirbelwind" alongside a Flakpanzer IV "Möbelwagen" at an ordnance collection point. The vehicle has been stripped of its weaponry. Note, as opposed to the vehicle on the previous page, the prominent zimmerit pattern which remained from the original Pz.IV chassis. *(Panzerwrecks)*

A GI carrying an M1 Garand rifle passes an abandoned Flakpanzer IV Wirbelwind in Belgium during January 1945. Note the wire on the turret, intended to foliage for camouflage. *(NARA)*

A view of the left front of the Wirbelwind turret interior. The ammunition rack to hold 20-round magazines is welded to the turret side.

The elevating (right) and traversing hand wheel (left) of the Flakpanzer IV's Flakvierling 38 mount. The Wirbelwind turret was cramped, and no turret roof could be added as the smoke generated by the firing of the 4x 2 cm guns filled the fighting compartment. The stenicilled box contained the cleaning gear for the guns.

Two views of a damaged and captured Flakpanzer IV "Wirbelwind" during February 1945. Note that three of the four barrels' flash hiders are missing. The hull (from a Panzer IV Ausf. G), is coated with Zimmerit anti-magnetic mine paste. A welded wire step has been added at the midpoint of the turret. *(NARA)*

# 30мм FLAK 38/103
# JABOSCHRECK

As the amount and intensity of Allied fighter bomber attacks increased steadily during 1944, the Germans sought quick and cost-effective solutions to defend against the threat. To add firepower against strongly built attack aircraft, like the P-47 Thunderbolt and the IL-II Sturmovik, the Germans turned to the available 3cm MK 103 aircraft cannon. Designed by Rheinmetall-Borsig, the MK 103 was initially used aboard the Hs-129 ground attack aircraft but was generally replaced in air-to-air use by the lighter 3cm MK 108. Consequently, there were MK 103 cannons available to create the "Jaboschreck"—a fanciful name for a MK 103 lashed up to a slightly modified 2 cm Flak 38 mounting.

Deployed in small numbers beginning in mid-1944, the Jaboschreck was a troubled marriage of weapons systems. The 3 cm gun was too powerful for the 2 cm mount, and the pronounced muzzle flash and recoil interfered with the gun sight and negatively impacted accuracy. The ammunition feed system was changed from the 20-round magazines of the 2 cm gun to a belt-fed arrangement in the MK 103. A sizeable muzzle brake was added, along with barrel and gun mount strengthening modifications, and the sight was improved, but the Jaboschreck remained a weapon with more potential than actual performance—although the added destructive power of the 3 cm ammunition was undeniable. Late in the war, a four-barreled version of the 3 cm MK 103, known as the "3 cm Flakvierling" was built in small numbers. The practical rate of fire of the MK 103 in these AA configurations was about 250 rounds per minute.

The only known surviving example of a Jaboschreck is in the collection of the US Army Air Defense Artillery Museum at Fort Sill, Oklahoma, and there is also a complete Kügelblitz turret in the inventory of the German Anti-Aircraft School.

The Pz.IV "Kügelblitz" prototype was also fitted with the Flak 38/103, in a closed turret featuring a twin-mount. Although the turret was intended to be tested on the Pz.38 chassis, five prototypes were built on the Pz. IV chassis and at least one saw action at the end of the war.

The Flak 38/103 was fitted to a modified Flak 38 mount. The 3 cm gun was belt-fed (metal with disintegrating links), and this required that a large ammunition box be placed on the left side of the cannon.

A Steyr truck (2000A or possibly 1500A) belonging to Panzergrenadier Regiment 40 of the 17th Panzer Division, abandoned in Usti nad Orlici in Czechoslovakia. Note the hinged side walls of the modified cargo bed, necessary to accommodate the crew and equipment while handling the 3 cm gun. *(Marek Solar)*

# 37mm FLAK 36/37/43

By the mid-1930s the Germans had noted the rapidly advancing performance of military aircraft, and rightly suspected that their 2 cm flak weapons would become obsolete sooner rather than later. Early examples of the 3.7 cm Flak appeared during 1935, but the weapon was beset with teething problems with its delicate Zeiss Flakvisier 33 sight, automatic feed for the 37x263mm B ammunition, and heavy, complicated carriage. The Germans pressed on, and by 1936 the 3.7 cm Flak 36 had appeared with a much lighter single-axle carriage and a much higher rate of fire (about 160 rounds per minute). In 1937 the 3.7 cm Flak 37 debuted, combining all the other improvements with a greatly simplified sighting system, the Uhrwerks-visier (Flakvisier 37) made by Zeiss.

All of the 3.7 cm variants served throughout WWII, providing excellent coverage in the low-to-medium flak ranges (up to about 14,000 feet). The 3.7 cm Flak weapons fired a highly destructive 1.4-pound shell with a practical rate of fire of about 80 rounds per minute. Emplaced batteries contained a maximum of 12 guns, with a normal crew size of 6-7 men per gun.

The Flak 43 represented an improvement over previous 3.7 cm guns in that the new design greatly simplified production and could be built in about ¼ the time. A new gas-operated breech mechanism, coupled with new 8-round magazines boosted its rate of fire, with a practical rate approaching 200 rounds per minute. To keep pace with the performance of Allied ground attack aircraft, the Flak 43 offered faster traverse and elevation, and used a simplified gunsight (the Flakvisier 43). The twin gun 3.7cm Flakzwilling 43 was also quite successful, essentially doubling the Flak 43's firepower. Unfortunately for the flak crews, few of the 3.7cm twin guns were made, with less than 400 in service at any time during the last year of the war.

There were a wide variety of self-propelled mounts for the 3.7cm AA guns, notably the Sd.Kfz. 6/2 and the Sd.Kfz. 7/2 which carried the Flak 36/37 and was produced in great numbers. From 1943 these vehicles featured an armored cab to protect the crew, and late-war versions often used the Flak 43 variant. The Flakpanzer IV Möbelwagen was also equipped with the Flak 43 and was produced in comparatively large numbers as well (approximately 240).

The 3.7 cm flak guns were mounted on a wide variety of flatbed trucks, including the Büssing-NAG 4500A and Mercedes-Benz L4500, but ultimately there were never enough of the 3.7cm AA guns to counter the ever-growing threat from Allied fighter-bombers.

An early 3.7 cm Flak 43 in service with Army Group South in Russia during May 1944. Note the 8-round ammunition clips, loaded horizontally. An 8mm Lebel Mle 1886/93 R35 carbine can be seen in front of the flak position—apparently brought from France by the gun crew.

A close-up view of the combination flash hider and muzzle brake of the Flak 37. Note the Flakvisier 37 gunsight.

Protecting the Afrika Korps: the North African desert provided sunny skies and a clear field of fire for this highly successful 3.7 cm Flak 36/37 crew.

The life of a Flak 36/37 crew: cleaning and servicing the 3.7 cm gun and loading the 6-round ammunition clips. This crew is seen on the Eastern front, during the summer of 1943.

A pair of 3.7 cm Flak 36/37 guns captured after being refurbished. Note the details of the gunner's seat and the elevating/traverse hand wheels mounted in front of it.

A Flak 36/37 unlimbered and brought into action on the Eastern Front. The 3.7 cm shells were also quite useful against ground targets. Note that the man kneeling at the right rear uses a binocular 10x80 spotting scope.

A 3.7 cm Flak 36 in a rather soggy position in France during the autumn of 1944. Note the 6-round ammunition clips stacked alongside the gun. *(NARA)*

A 3.7 cm Flak 36 captured in standard flak bunker in France during 1944. Note that the gun has been raised up on blocks. Extra 6-round ammunition clips are stored beside the gun, as well as in dugout locations in the front and rear of the bunker. *(NARA)*

The 3.7 cm Flak 36 This example was captured aboard its Sonder Anhanger trailer in Germany during early 1945. Ammunition was fed via 6-round clips, with a practical cyclic rate of 80 rpm. (NARA)

The 3.7 cm Flakzwilling 43 in travelling position on the four-wheel Sonder An-hänger 106 carriage. *(NARA)*

Doubling the 3.7cm firepower: The guns of the Flakzwilling 43 were mounted one above the other in the same vertical plane. Maximum elevation was 90 degrees. *(NARA)*

Summer in Russia: Time for a beer and a short break for this crew of a Sd. Kfz. 6/2. The attached Sd. Ah 52 trailer carries the ammunition and equipment box for the 3.7 cm Flak 36, as well as most of the crew's gear. The trailer payload was about 3,750 pounds.

The 3.7 cm Flak 36 of a Sd. Kfz. 6/2 covers a river crossing in Russia during the spring of 1942.

A 3.7 cm Flak 37 mounted on a five-ton Daimler-Benz L-4500R "Maultier". The man in the foreground uses a binocular 10x80 spotting scope.

With the short folding sides up, the 3,7 cm Flak 36 seems quite cramped on the deck of the Sd. Kfz. 6/2.

Two views of a Selbstfahrlafette mit 3.7 cm Flak 36 (Sd. Kfz. 7/2) knocked out in Italy during the late spring of 1944. Note the details of the 37mm ammunition canisters and the damage to the lightly armored cab, probably caused by .50 caliber machine gun fire. *(Panzerwrecks and NARA)*

WL-427228

This Sd. Kfz. 7/2 was captured by the US Third Army in Germany during early April 1945. This vehicle carries the later 3.7 cm Flak 43. Nearly 1000 Sd. Kfz. 7/2s were built by January 1945. The cab is lightly armored (7/16th-inch thick) and the radiator is protected by a V-shaped armored shield. The crew was normally comprised of seven men. *(NARA)*

A view of the lightly armored cab of a Sd. Kfz. 7/2 knocked out in northern France during the autumn of 1944. The GI at right points out a large caliber shell hole that penetrated the thin armored shield on the vehicle's radiator. *(NARA)*

Germany's efforts to provide effective defense for its armored formations from the growing number of Allied ground attack aircraft yielded the Flakpanzer IV "Möbelwagen"— which coupled mobility and some armor protection with the highly-effective 3.7 cm Flak 43. (*David Doyle*)

The easily folding walls of the Flakpanzer IV superstructure were made of two 15mm plates, spaced at 55mm for the sides, and 50mm for the front and rear. The 3.7cm Flak 43 was fully automatic, gas-operated, and clip-fed from a side tray. Traverse was 360 degrees,with 17 ½ revolutions of the hand wheel, and 90 degrees elevation with 12 revolutions of the hand wheel. (David Doyle)

The Flakpanzer IV "Möbelwagen" was a simple, cost-effective design with about 240 built, beginning in March 1944. This example is one the later (past the first 45) production models with simplified, straight-edge side plates. Note the pistol port at the rear right, the pivoting armored cover was 25mm thick. *(Panzerwrecks)*

This Flakpanzer IV "Mobelwagen" was captured in Normandy, and was one of the first of its kind to be examined by US Ordnance Technical Intelligence.

Opposite page: Details of the 3.7 cm Flak 43 cannon of the Flakpanzer IV shown on Page 108. Note the elongated ammunition feed tray and details of the gun. The gunner's position was described as particularly cramped, noting:
"A large man would find it impossible to track evenly and fire the gun."

GIs examine a Flakpanzer IV "Möbelwagen", which was captured in Hosingen, Germany, near the Siegfried Line during February 1945. The vehicle must have suffered from a direct hit, judging from the cracked armoured side wall. *(NARA)*

The Flakpanzer IV "Ostwind". Production of this vehicle, armed with the 3.7 cm Flak 43, began in March 1944, but only 44 were completed by the end of the war. The Ostwind featured heavier armor on its octagonal turret (increased to 25mm) than its predecessor "Wirbelwind". Note that the hull is covered in Zimmerit anti-magnetic mine paste. *(David Doyle)*

# 50mm FLAK 41

In order to fill the "flak gap" between the 3,7 cm and 8,8 cm guns, Germany created the ill-fated 5 cm Flak 41. Rheinmetall built a short run of fifty guns during late 1940, and within a year of extensive troop trials the Flak 41 fell far short of expectations. Although mobile (on the Sonder Anhanger 204 trailer), the 5 cm gun was found to be unstable due to extremely heavy recoil, the muzzle flash was blinding for the gunners and gave away its position, and the weapon traversed too slowly to effectively track fast-moving aircraft. The Flak 41 fired a 4.8-pound shell and had a cyclic rate of about 150 rounds per minute. Ammunition was fed via 5-round clips. Despite its limited production and the overall disappointing performance of the weapon, the Flak 41 soldiered on, and a good amount of the production run were still in service during 1944.

A Flak 41 captured by US troops. The gun is seen aboard the Sonder Anhänger 204 carriage. *(Panzerwrecks)*

A 5 cm Flak 41 in position. Note that there are two 5-round ammunition clips ready to feed into the gun.

# 85/88ᴍᴍ FLAK M39(ʀ)

Germany used many captured AA guns during the war—most of them confined to secondary roles due to their odd ammunition types. However, the Soviet 85mm AA gun Model 1939 proved itself to be an outstanding weapon, close in performance to the German 88mm types. A large amount of the 85mm Model 1939 guns were captured in the first 18 months of the German invasion of the Soviet Union. As the supply of captured 85mm ammunition began to run out, many of these guns were taken to the Reich to bolster strategic flak defenses, and were rebored to accept 88mm ammunition, becoming the 8.5/8.8 cm Flak M.39 (r). These guns fired a 20.2-pound shell at 10 rounds per minute to an effective ceiling of about 34,000 feet.

As Allied troops pressed further into the Reich, they encountered increasing numbers of the Soviet-made M39 85mm AA guns, many of them rebored to use German 88mm ammunition. *(NARA)*

A 85/88mm Flak M39(r) captured by US troops in the spring of 1945. *(NARA)*

# 88MM FLAK 18/36/37/41

The German 88mm guns received so much notoriety in the anti-tank role, that their abilities as anti-aircraft weapons are often overlooked. Regardless of their success against ground targets, the 88mm family of guns represented some of the deadliest flak weapons of all time. The 88mm gun entered service in 1917 as the "8.8 cm K.Zugflak L/45" (often abbreviated to K-Flak). The K-Flak used a semi-automatic, sliding wedge breech designed by Krupp, giving the weapon a respectable rate of fire of 10 rounds per minute. With a vertical range of up to 22,000 feet, and a shell weight of 20.75 pounds, the K-Flak was a highly effective weapon by WWI standards.

After a flirtation with a 75mm design (the 7.5 cm Flak L/60), the Germans renewed their 88mm development and the result was the 8.8 cm Flak 18, which was an unqualified success. The Flak 18 first saw action during the Spanish Civil War and remained a dominant weapon system throughout WWII. A big part of the 88mm's ability to deal with targets on the ground and in the air came from its mobility—the Sonder Anhanger 201/202 carriage coupled with a cruciform platform allowed for tremendous flexibility and positioning with a powerful gun. The Flak 18 had a semi-automatic breech and used a mechanical fuse-setter. Its fire control came via a central transmission system, and its pedestal mount was equipped with leveling controls. The maximum ceiling was 32,000 feet, with an effective ceiling of 26,000. The normal crew was made up of a gun commander and nine men.

The Flak 36 was almost identical to the Flak 18, and the Flak 37 quite similar, with the exception that its new data transmission system. All three variants combined to create the backbone of Germany's AA defense throughout WWII.

From an anti-aircraft perspective, the best of all the 88mm guns came in the form of the Flak 41, first conceived in 1939, and finally debuted in 1943. Originally designed as a dual-purpose AT/AA weapon, the Flak 41 used a turntable carriage instead of the usual pedestal mount of its predecessors. Troublesome complexities, like a separate firing circuit for ground use, and the need for continuous skilled maintenance made the Flak 41 less than desirable in the field. However, the gun's fantastic performance in the AA role (firing at up to 25 rpm) meant that all available examples were returned to the Reich and emplaced near strategic targets. The Flak 41 was expensive to produce, and its need for specialized service obscured what was one of the finest flak weapons of the entire war. Its maximum ceiling was 49,215 feet—highest of all the German flak guns.

While the 8,8 cm guns gained considerable fame as anti-tank weapons, they were ultimately Germany's most reliable and effective anti-aircraft weapons. (SA-Kuva)

8,8 cm ammunition was often shipped in wood and wicker containers containing three rounds. The cover and base of the container are metal. The cover is held in place by a leather strap. The dimensions of the wicker container are 38.5x14.75x5.5 inches.

The 8,8 cm Flak 18: The pride of the pre-war flak artillery, and in service throughout World War II. These were photographed at a garrison in Schweinfurt. *(Petr Dolezal)*

The usual flak bunker for the 8,8 cm gun had two entrances to ease emplacement and extraction. Ready ammunition was stored in the walls of the dugout. Crew bunkers, search lights, and a command post were close by in the battery position, often connected via a trench system.

The Flak 18 introduced the concept of a heavy yet highly mobile anti-aircraft gun. When towed aboard the Sd. Ah. 201 carriage, the 8,8 cm could be fired from the wheels as soon as the folded outrigger arms were dropped and secured. *(Panzerwrecks)*

Battery positions for the flak guns varied in the quality of their preparation, but many began to take on some home-like qualities. Note the wooden bench against the far wall of the dugout.

Cleaning the casing of an 8,8 cm round before loading into a Flak 18 on the Eastern Front.

Serving an 8,8 cm gun required a crew of up to 11 men: commander, 2x gun operators, 2x fuse setters, a loader, 4x ammo assistants, and a driver for the towing vehicle. Note the two rounds placed in the fuse setter.

A quiet moment for a Luftwaffe gun crew on the Eastern Front, their 8,8 cm cannon could be in action at a moment's notice against enemy aircraft or tanks. The 88 was a particularly feared weapon when operating on open ground. *(Petr Dolezal)*

A German crew (probably Coastal Artillery of the Kriegsmarine judging from the shoulder clasps) operating the 8.8 cm Flak 18/2, mounted on a pedestal on the Island of Tytärsaari, Finland. Note the ammunition stored in the walls of the far side of the bunker. *(SA-Kuva)*

The expected barrel life of a 8.8 cm Flak 18 was approximately 900 rounds. However, there was always the chance of an unfortunate surprise. Note the crew's helmets lined up on the earthen shelf of this rough-hewn gun bunker. *(Petr Dolezal)*

Ramming home the shell into the gun's breech, the loader wears an asbestos mitt to avoid being burned. To his left, a round is inserted into the fuse setter.

A detailed look at the 8.8 cm breech, with the two gun operators to the right. One of the fuse setters sits with his back against the gun shield, while the loader (wearing his asbestos glove) considers the remnants of his lunch in a M31 mess tin.

GIs examine one of their most feared opponents near Augsburg, Germany during May 1945. This gun was captured in its static mount-fixed emplacement. When emplaced in a static mount, the guns were given "2" suffix to denote the pedestal mount— Flak 18/2, Flak 36/2, Flak 37/2, and Flak 41/2.

Opposite page: Captured 8,8 cm guns provided Allied troops with prized opportunities for a trophy photo. The GI at right uses his M1A1 Thompson SMG to point out the Flak 36's spiked barrel (Valognes, France during July 1944).

Towed by a Sd. Kfz. 7 on a Sd. Ah. 201 carriage, this Flak 18 advances over the rough roads of the Eastern Front.

A good view of the Sd. Ah. 202. The main difference between the Sd.Ah. 201 and 202 was the forward carriage, which on the latter featured two wheels side by side, similar to the rear carriage. The mudguards were also more rounded, rather than wave-shaped. See page 128 for a direct comparison. *(Petr Dolezal)*

An 8.8 cm Flak 36 (with Flak-Rohr 18) set up in Finland. Note the wicker ammunition containers (three rounds each) in the foreground, along with the front bogie wheels of the Sd. Ah. 202. (SA-Kuva)

The end in North Africa: A pair of Flak 36 captured in Tunisia during 1943. Note the details of the Sd. Ah. 202's twin tires. (NARA)

Changing tires on the Sd. Ah. 201 single axle bogie. Tires were always at premium in German armed forces, but particularly so in the North African campaign. Note the details on the folded up outrigger and the canvas breech cover (essential to keep out the grains of sand).

This Flak 36 was abandoned by German troops in Finland and is seen being towed off a transport vessel. Note the interesting wave camouflage and muzzle cover. *(SA-Kuva)*

This Flak 37 met its destiny in a field in Normandy. The carriage was probably moved after it was knocked out, since the grass seems fresh around the burnt wheels. Note the scorched paint on the front fenders and barrel. *(NARA)*

Troops of the US 79th Infantry Division inspect a 8.8 cm Flak 36, captured at Fougeres, France, on August 7, 1944. *(NARA)*

Examining a captured 8.8 cm Flak 41 in Italy during 1943. If the kill markings painted on the side of the gun shield are to believed, this particular weapon was highly effective against Allied bombers. *(NARA)*

Examining a captured 8.8 cm Flak 41. While the advanced designed proved finicky and troublesome in the field, when the Flak 41's were sent to the Reich, they shined as the best of all the German AA guns. Note the details of the Sonderhanger 202 carriage and the low silhouette of the Flak 41's turnstile mounting. *(Panzerwrecks)*

A GI examines an 8.8 cm Flak 41. This gun was thoroughly wrecked by the Germans before its capture—the entire breech block and loading mechanism have been blown off. Note the ammunition canisters in the foreground. *(NARA)*

Germany's shallow-draft Siebel ferries were constructed of two pontoons connected by a bridge. Armament was up to four 8,8 cm guns, along with several 2 cm Flak weapons. Highly versatile craft, they could operate on rivers, lakes, and in seacoast areas. Note the MG34 on a pedestal in the image at left, and the multiple kill markings on the gun at right. *(SA-Kuva)*

Flak 18s being fitted on the deck of a Sibel ferry. These ferries operated on Lake Ladoga, and were interestingly manned by Luftwaffe crews rather than Kriegsmarine. (*SA-Kuva*)

A good view of the placement of the two 8,8 cm guns. Note the five-meter coastal range finder on the armored bridge at top right. *(SA-Kuva)*

The crew of an 8,8 cm gun mounted on a Siebel Ferry prepares ammunition for their next fire mission in Finnish waters. The discs on the makeshift table are the covers from the steel containers for the individual Flak 18/37 rounds. (SA-Kuva)

A Luftwaffe gun crew cleaning the breech actuator and rammer guard of an 8.8 cm Flak 18 mounted on a Siebel Ferry in Finland. *(SA-Kuva)*

88mm rounds were packed in individual sealed steel containers (painted slate gray), or three per wicker basket. The container is hermetically sealed with a rubber gasket under the removable steel cover. The weight of one round in a steel container is approximately 47 pounds. (SA-Kuva)

A beautiful detail photo of the Flak 18's breech and loading tray. The elevating wheel is at the bottom right. (SA-Kuva)

140

"Eisenbahnflak": Many 8,8 cm guns were mounted on rail cars ("Geschützwagen") so they could be shuttled around the Reich to concentrate flak assets where they were needed the most. The guns were placed on pedestal mounts with their outrigger arms removed. The gun crews lived aboard the train with all the necessary support material for the guns. This Geschutzwagen III has concrete walls added to protect the crew. *(NARA)*

# 105MM FLAK 39 / 128MM FLAK 40

By the mid 1930s, the flight performance of modern bombers was increasing dramatically, particularly in the altitudes the aircraft could reach. Consequently, German designers began working on weapons that could hit enemy bombers at heights beyond the capabilities of the standard 8,8 cm Flak guns. On first glance the 10.5 cm Flak 38 appears to be little more than a scaled-up 8,8 cm Flak 18. In fact, the new Flak 38 used an innovative electrical fire control and loading system. Before WWII began certain improvements were made, including updated electronics and a sectioned gun barrel, and the revised system was designated the 10.5 cm Flak 39. The normal 10-man crew would be upped to 12 if the weapon's loader was operated manually.

The 10.5 cm guns became an important part of the German heavy flak batteries—many were placed in static mounts to defend strategic targets, while some were carried on special "flak train" railway mounts. Unlike the later 12.8 cm Flak 40 guns, the Flak 38/39 could be towed into position on the Sonder Anhanger 201 trailer, and many of these guns were deployed in that fashion.

The Flak 38/39 (chambered in 105x769mm R) fired a 33.3-pound shell up to a maximum ceiling of 42,000 feet. About 4,200 were built.

### STRATEGIC FLAK: THE 12.8 CM FLAK 40

Development of the Flak 40 began in 1936, and the gun was ultimately designed and built by Rheinmetall-Borsig. An advanced weapon for its time, the Flak 40 featured a hydro-pneumatic recoil system, and the shells were fed into the breech with a power rammer. It was first introduced during 1942, as Allied heavy bombers began to operate with greater frequency over the Reich.

The Flak 40 was a massive weapon system, and at nearly 17 tons the gun could not be easily moved cross country. Consequently, it was often mounted in specially designed "flak towers" to protect strategically important areas. This was particularly true for the twin-gun "12.8 cm Flakzwilling 40"—the Flakzwilling guns fired twenty rounds per minute and provided formidable AA defense for cities like Berlin and Hamburg. However, the Flakzwilling guns were few, and by the winter of 1945 there were just 34 of the massive twin 12.8 cm guns in service. As for the single barrel guns, there were about 360 in fixed emplacements, with a further 200 mounted on rail cars during February 1945.

The Germans created special flak trains to give the Flak 40 and its crew of ten men, a measure of mobility, shuttling the big guns to where they were needed the most—about 200 of the guns were mounted on special rail cars. Guns in static positions were bolted into concrete firing platforms.

The Flak 40 was an extremely effective gun but the high cost of production meant that only about 1,100 guns made by 1945. The massive 128x958mm R rounds used nearly four times the powder of a standard 88mm flak shell. The 128mm shell weighed 57.3 pounds and could reach a maximum of 48,500 feet. The maximum rate of fire for the Flak 40 was 12 rounds per minute.

While the 10.5 cm guns could be carried on the Sonder Anhänger 201 trailer, many were grouped into special "flak trains" and shuttled between strategic targets.

A Flak 39 10.5 cm anti-aircraft gun emplaced at a coastal defense battery during 1942.

Opposite left:
Ammunition for the heavy flak guns:
From 8.8 cm to 12.8 cm.

The Flak 39 10.5 cm looked like an enlarged 8,8 cm Flak 18, but used an electrical fire control and loading mechanism, along with a sectional barrel.

144

A Flak 39 abandoned on the remains of its Sonder Anhanger 201 trailer. *(NARA)*

The Flak 39 10.5 cm guns were emplaced to dominate strategically important areas. These guns are seen in sunny Italy. At left, a GI examines the massive 10.5 cm ammunition.

The same 10,5 cm Flak 38 seen on the previous page. Note the details of the loading/firing system.

A 12.8 cm 40/2 anti-aircraft gun captured outside Gelsenkirchen. The barrel and breech were disabled by the crew. In this position, the 12.8 cm gun could also serve as an anti-tank gun. *(NARA)*

This 12.8 cm 40/2 gun was captured by US troops near Leuna. The image provides excellent details of a round in the fuse-setter, as well as ammunition storage in walls of the gun bunker. *(NARA)*

The remains of a shattered flak train, hit by USAAF fighter bombers and captured by US troops in Germany during the late spring of 1945. There are three 12.8 cm Flak 40 guns visible on this train. *(NARA)*

Special railcar mountings gave the massive (28,665-pounds) Flak 40 good mobility.  In the winter of 1945, there were still approximately 200 of the 12.8 cm AA guns operating on railways.